BI-POLAR GIRL

An Irreverent Look at Bipolar Disorder

GABRIELLE BLACKMAN-SHEPPARD

Illustrated by Greg Blackman

Edited by Ian Gilbert

Crown House Publishing Ltd
www.crownhouse.co.uk
www.crownhousepublishing.com

First published by
Crown House Publishing Ltd
Crown Buildings, Bancyfelin, Carmarthen, Wales, SA33 5ND, UK
www.crownhouse.co.uk

and

Crown House Publishing Company LLC
6 Trowbridge Drive, Suite 5, Bethel, CT 06801, USA
www.crownhousepublishing.com

British Library of Cataloguing-in-Publication Data
A catalogue entry for this book is available
from the British Library.

10-digit ISBN 184590446-X
13-digit ISBN 978-184590446-3

LCCN 2010931720

Printed and bound in the UK by
Bell and Bain Ltd, Glasgow

To my father

FOREWORD

We all have moods. We all have good days and bad days. We all have times when we feel unstoppable and we have times when we just want to stop and make it all go away. That's perfectly normal. After all, we are all just perfectly normal human beings, aren't we ...

But what happens when our 'ups' are just a little bit, well, too up? When we don't just feel unstoppable but we feel invincible and when nothing could ever bring us down? We can do what we want, eat what we want, spend what we want, work hard, play hard and tomorrow, we know for certain, will simply never come. In fact, we are so 'up', we haven't really noticed that we can't come down.

Until that day when we do. With a crash.

When that happens, we aren't just a bit down, we are seriously can't get out of bed, don't draw the curtains, make the world go away, I don't care if you are my partner or my parent or my child, just leave me alone and switch off the light very down indeed.

Highs and lows are normal. To experience the highest highs and the lowest lows means there is something more sinister going on in our brains. This is the realm of bipolar disorder.

This is what this book is all about.

For a long time referred to with the catch-all title of 'manic depression', bipolar disorder is becoming better understood these days but even so, like all mental illness, it is still the subject of a great deal of misunderstanding, confusion, fear, blame, and guilt. And, like all mental illness, there is a lot of it about. According to the UK's Mental Health Foundation, 'one in four people will experience some kind of mental health problem in the course of the year'[1] (with women more likely to be treated than men). In other words, if you don't suffer from some form of mental illness, someone close to you probably will.

There are a number of ways to treat a condition such as bipolar disorder. Medication is one, with any number of drugs available but a lottery as to which one will work, how, when, and with what side effects. Diet and exercise play their part too. Alcohol is a depressant even though you start off by feeling good. Exercise helps us produce serotonin, the lack of which can lead to depression. There's another treatment too that can not only help someone with the condition, it may also help to prevent it too. It's called honesty.

In the remarkably frank and vivid portrayal of a woman whose life comes crashing down as a result of bipolar disorder, Gabrielle takes the reader on the mental roller coaster that is her illness and, if not the cure, the treatment that follows her diagnosis. And she does so with an honesty that is rarely found in a subject that is denied, hidden, maligned, and treated as a taboo (the World Health Organization quotes a public survey which revealed that most people put mental disorder down to stress or 'lack of willpower').[2]

Whether you read this book because you are coming to terms with your own illness or searching within it for a better understanding of the illness of a loved one, I know that Gabrielle's honesty will be of support to you on your own roller-coaster journey. All we ask of you in return is that you too talk about the illness and your experiences with equal honesty and do your bit to help others in the way that we hope Gabrielle has helped you.

Ian Gilbert
Suffolk
10 October 2010 – World Mental Health Day

PREFACE

This little book was born out of my desire to encourage those poor souls who find themselves sitting in the waiting rooms of psychiatric clinics and hospitals.

Bi-Polar Girl is a personal story based on my real-life experience of living with bipolar disorder. It is not meant to be a recommendation for any particular treatment.

Bipolar disorder, also known as manic-depressive illness, is a brain disorder that causes unusual shifts in mood, energy, activity levels, and the ability to carry out day-to-day tasks. Symptoms of bipolar disorder are severe. They are different from the normal ups and downs that everyone goes through from time to time. Bipolar disorder symptoms can result in damaged relationships, poor job or school performance, and even suicide. But bipolar disorder can be treated, and people with this illness can lead full and productive lives.

Bi-Polar Girl eventually found her way back to a happy life, full of love, hope, and laughter.

May YOU find your way back to laughter and the life YOU want to live.

For more support visit my blog www.bi-polargirl.com

ACKNOWLEDGEMENTS

It is impossible for me to acknowledge here all those kind souls who have helped me on my journey and who have encouraged me to write this little book.

I thank you all from the bottom of my heart and I hope by now that you all know who you are!

I must however give special thanks to my son Greg for his wonderful illustrations without which Bi-Polar Girl would have a voice but no face. He knows bipolar disorder from his personal experience as well as from my own.

I must also thank my friend and coach Lynette Allen whose financial generosity and boundless belief in me has fed my confidence and kept my dream alive.

Last, but not least, a massive thank you to my editor Ian Gilbert for his generous understanding and patience.

To you all I am grateful.

CONTENTS

Chapter 1
GREETINGS

How it all Started

What would help YOU feel less
scared right now?

What would help YOU feel there IS light
at the end of YOUR tunnel?

You are probably feeling very scared right now. I know I was.

You are also probably finding it impossible to believe you will ever get better. I know I did.

It helped me to have someone else understand what I was going through. It made a big difference for me to know that other people still believed in me when I no longer believed in myself.

I hope that following the 'adventures' of Bi-Polar Girl will help you feel less frightened and less lonely.

I have been where you are at this moment and I am right here with you.

BI-POLAR GIRL

What mental illness do YOU have:

Bipolar disorder I?

Bipolar disorder II?

Hello! My name is Bi-Polar Girl.

I have bipolar disorder (BPD) II.

Maybe you have BPD II like me or maybe you have BPD I.

BPD I has high peaks (full manic episodes) and deep valleys (severe clinical depression).

BPD II has high wide plateaus (a hypo-manic state that lasts a long time) and deep wide canyons (severe and prolonged clinical depression).

Whichever way, you and I inhabit the same mental health territory.

When YOU look back at your past life:

What do YOU see?

What do YOU learn?

Greetings

Come with me. Together we will look back at what brought ME to where YOU are now.

My journey is also your journey.

Are you happy for me to be your companion for the rest of this little book?

Yes? Then follow me.

What is it that tells YOU things
aren't quite right for YOU?

Greetings

It all started one day when Bi-Polar Girl found that she could not get out of bed. Her body felt like concrete and she could not keep her eyes open.

Bi-Polar Girl thought, 'I must be very tired.' A week later and still stuck in her concrete body with her concrete-heavy eyelids, she thought, 'I feel so bad I wish I were dead.'

Something was not right ... She thought she had better go to the doctor's.

**What other health problems
have YOU discovered that were in fact
caused by clinical depression?**

Bi-Polar Girl went to see her GP and she had various blood tests to find out what was wrong with her.

Because the glands in her neck were swollen, the doctor thought Bi-Polar Girl might have glandular fever or a really bad virus but all the tests came back negative.

A few weeks later and feeling a bit better, Bi-Polar Girl thought no more of it and tried to resume her normal activities.

What has convinced YOU that you are suffering from clinical depression?

Very soon Bi-Polar Girl started to feel exhausted again. This time the fatigue would not go away. Bi-Polar Girl felt like she was melting into a big black hole that was sucking up all her energy. This time her doctor diagnosed serious clinical depression.

Bi-Polar Girl was so stubborn that she refused to accept she had become seriously ill with depression.

It took her GP and a very good friend (who was also a psych iatrist) to convince her to seek psychiatric treatment.

What is YOUR view of
clinical depression?

Greetings

Until now Bi-Polar Girl had always been very good at putting on a brave face and pulling herself together.

Because she was a strong, enthusiastic person with a very positive outlook, Bi-Polar Girl did not understand how she could possibly be suffering from depression.

Bi-Polar Girl thought clinical depression was not a 'real' illness and depression was a weak, negative disorder to have.

She was so ill though that all her usual techniques and coping mechanisms were failing her. She grew desperate enough to see the psychiatrist to whom she had been referred.

The psychiatrist told Bi-Polar Girl she was very ill and needed immediate treatment because she had BPD II.

Chapter 2
BEFORE THE CRASH

Spiralling Upwards

What kind of person would YOU say YOU
were before you became ill?

Bi-Polar Girl was an enthusiastic person.

She loved music. She loved dancing. She had a zest for life.

Bi-Polar Girl put a lot of energy and passion into *everything* she did.

She saw herself as an optimistic go-getter who got a kick out of making things happen.

Everybody admired her energy.

What important internal
knowledge do YOU ignore?

Bi-Polar Girl was not a sad person either. She was quick to smile, she liked to laugh, and she was known for her wicked sense of humour.

She was not easily discouraged and rarely despondent.

Bi-Polar Girl was a positive thinker; she was a glass over-flowing kind of girl.

Deep inside she had always had a sense that something in her was 'fragile' but she had always ignored it.

What does YOUR schedule look like:

Daily?

Weekly?

Monthly?

Bi-Polar Girl was always in forward-planning mode.

Her days were full and she spent a lot of time filling up her calendar to the maximum.

She never had enough time to do all the things she wanted to do. She lived with a constant sense that there were not enough hours in the day, enough days in the week, and enough weeks in the month.

Bi-Polar Girl routinely scheduled enough work in any one day to keep two people busy!

How far ahead do YOU normally look?

Bi-Polar Girl was also a great goal setter.

She liked nothing better than to set herself some tough targets.

Big-Polar Girl was self-motivated and internally driven. She did not need much supervision or much coaxing.

She was known for being organised and efficient and she was proud of her reputation.

What proportion of your time and energy
do YOU invest in YOUR work?

Bi-Polar Girl's capacity for working long hours was encouraged by her boss and her colleagues who expected more and more from her.

As a result, she felt stuck on a treadmill she could not stop.

Bi-Polar Girl got used to thinking of her work and her career as a 'do or die' situation.

She saw it as a test of her mettle and she strived continuously to rise to the challenge.

How much of a perfectionist are YOU?

Bi-Polar Girl was a bit of a perfectionist.

She did everything to the highest standard she could muster.

She put a lot of thought and energy into every task, at work and at home.

Bi-Polar Girl was the sort of person who ironed trouser pleats in her husband's pyjamas!

What proportion of YOUR time and energy do YOU invest in YOUR home life?

How responsible do YOU feel for other people in your life?

Not only did Bi-Polar Girl work long hours in the office but she also felt driven to do a good job on the home front.

She put a lot of effort and energy into keeping the house clean and tidy.

She put more effort and energy into cooking nutritious meals for her family.

Bi-Polar Girl felt responsible for everyone around her.

How tough are the goals YOU
set for YOURSELF?

Everything Bi-Polar Girl did was done with purpose, enthusiasm, and energy.

She knew what she wanted and she worked hard to get it.

She knew where she was going and she was prepared to walk long distances to get there.

She knew what she expected of herself and she never let herself off the hook.

She knew. Or so she thought ...

How fast are YOU living YOUR life?

As time went by Bi-Polar Girl lived at a faster and faster pace.

She felt like she was driving herself at 100 miles per hour and she became intoxicated by her own speed.

Even her language started to feel rushed.

Bi-Polar Girl had so many racing thoughts in her head that her mouth had trouble keeping up!

How much quiet reflection time do YOU
allow YOURSELF on a regular basis?

Gradually, Bi-Polar Girl became unable to reflect or think quietly about anything.

Her internal voice was constantly shouting and urging her on.

The pressure was building up inside her but Bi-Polar Girl thought this was a test of her grit and determination.

As her internal voice grew louder Bi-Polar Girl became her own tyrant – she started treating herself like a slave.

How strong and tough do YOU
think you are?

Bi-Polar Girl reached the stage where she felt invincible.

There was nothing she could not achieve.

Her natural enthusiasm and passion had become rocket fuel propelling her ever upwards, ever forwards.

She felt so bright.

She felt so strong.

And she liked it.

In what way do YOU get reckless:

Spending money?

Engaging in sexual promiscuity?

Exhibiting other high risk behaviour?

Bi-Polar Girl's dreams became BIG goals.

There was no limit to what she was prepared to borrow and spend to make those dreams come true.

Her debts were mounting up and yet Bi-Polar Girl felt as wealthy as an oil tycoon.

She had always been cautious with money but now she became obsessed with the idea that she needed to speculate in order to accumulate.

How much pressure do YOU
put YOURSELF under?

As if she didn't have enough on her over-loaded plate, Bi-Polar Girl started a strict diet and exercise regime.

She lost a lot of weight and she felt on top of the world.

Bi-Polar Girl had more and more energy and she was constantly buzzing.

She became addicted to this buzzing feeling and always wanted more of it.

She *appeared* to be thriving under continuous pressure ...

What happens to YOUR sleeping pattern?

Bi-Polar Girl was sleeping less and less.

There came a point when she was hardly sleeping at all. She had difficulty getting two hours of sleep a night.

Bi-Polar Girl could work through the day, through the night, and through another day seemingly without any problems.

She did not feel sleepy.

She did not even feel tired.

When YOUR illness is escalating,
what experiences do YOU have that
touch YOUR soul?

Bi-Polar Girl started to feel as if she was in touch with God Himself. She could feel His presence all around her.

She could feel angels' wings brushing by her.

She could feel Heaven.

It was the most deliciously blissful feeling she had ever experienced!

Bi-Polar Girl thought this was such a beautiful place that she did not want to leave it – ever.

Chapter 3

THE POINT OF NO RETURN

Sliding Downwards

Have YOU ever reached YOUR
Point of No Return?

If/when you did what happened to YOU?

But then one day Bi-Polar Girl suddenly felt anxious for no apparent reason.

A sense of dread and impending doom started to take over her whole body.

Bi-Polar Girl felt as if an intense threat was just around the corner and yet she could not identify it.

She tried to shrug off her anxiety but it would NOT go away.

So Bi-Polar Girl fought her creeping fear with feelings of aggression and hostility. She had reached her Point of No Return.

How do YOU feel when YOU
lose control of YOUR life?

One day, as her fear continued to grow, Bi-Polar Girl realised that her reckless spending and ill-advised investing had left her with nothing.

She was broke.

Worse still, she was bankrupt.

Losing all her money was very frightening to Bi-Polar Girl. She had grown up watching her parents struggle financially and she was scared of being penniless.

Her fear and anxiety became overwhelming. Bi-Polar Girl coped by feeling more aggression and hostility.

What 'break–down' signals is YOUR
body giving YOU?

One day Bi-Polar Girl found she could no longer do her usual work.

She felt as if something inside her had ceased to function.

Bi-Polar Girl felt stuck.

She could not understand what was wrong. She was fit and apparently physically healthy and yet her body refused to respond properly to her brain's commands.

Bi-Polar Girl's 'machinery' was starting to let her down.

How ashamed do YOU
feel about your illness?

How isolated do YOU feel as a result?

Bi-Polar Girl was afraid. Worse still, she also felt ashamed.

She hated not being able to do the best work she was capable of. She hated feeling less committed to excellence.

Bi-Polar Girl was certain she would lose her reputation if other people knew what was happening to her. She was afraid she would also lose her job. So she said nothing.

Bi-Polar Girl had always been gregarious and a real 'people person' but she suddenly felt utterly alone.

What is YOUR deepest fear?

How does it show up in YOUR illness?

One day Bi-Polar Girl lost her sense of connection with all that is good and beautiful in this world.

It was gradually replaced by the feeling that she was now connected to all that is dark and dangerous.

To Bi-Polar Girl, it felt as if her very soul was under attack. She screamed and screamed into her pillow at night.

She started to wonder whether she was losing her mind ...

How exhausted do YOU feel?

How much do YOU worry about it?

One day Bi-Polar Girl found she had trouble waking up. After such a long time with so little sleep, this new sleepiness felt very strange.

Bi-Polar Girl started feeling more and more exhausted.

She thought she had caught a virus and did her best to struggle on.

She worried about her work piling up.

She worried about her body aching all over.

For the first time in her life Bi-Polar Girl worried a great deal.

How precarious does YOUR balance feel?

How afraid are YOU of losing it
altogether?

One day Bi-Polar Girl felt as if everything was shrinking around her.

Nothing worked as it should. Every little thing had become a huge struggle.

Her body no longer felt like her own.

Bi-Polar Girl was gradually losing her precarious balance.

It seemed she was using all the energy she had left to stop herself from falling over.

Do YOU feel your life is unravelling?

What do YOU do to try to stop it?

Suddenly Bi-Polar Girl felt like her life was unravelling and, even though she tried very hard, she could not knit it back together again.

She tried everything she could think of.

She used all her professional and personal development training but Bi-Polar Girl could no longer knit fast enough to hold herself together.

Bi-Polar Girl felt like she too had started to unravel ...

What do YOU refuse to acknowledge
even when YOU feel really ill?

One morning Bi-Polar Girl found she could not get herself ready for work.

She had always been well turned out and taken pride in her appearance.

But now she felt a mess and she looked a mess.

She kidded herself she had a viral flu and finally took two weeks of sick leave.

In spite of how ill she was feeling, Bi-Polar Girl also felt very guilty about taking time off work.

What do YOU do when YOU
feel small inside?

Bi-Polar Girl could not recognise herself.

She continued expecting herself to be the way she used to be: big and strong.

But now she felt weak and small.

The outside world wasn't the only thing that was shrinking: she was shrinking too.

In spite of everything, Bi-Polar Girl still refused to see what was staring her in the face ...

What kind of hole do YOU
dig for YOURSELF?

Even though she was still feeling very unwell Bi-Polar Girl went back to work.

She ignored all the warning signs her body had been giving her and did her best to resume her activities.

Bi-Polar Girl thought she was being strong – but she was wrong.

She was just digging a big hole for herself.

What would YOU realise if YOU
took a bird's eye view of YOUR life?

Bi-Polar Girl forgot to look at her life's big picture.

During her time off work she could have taken a step back and looked at the life she was living.

But Bi-Polar Girl kept her nose to the grindstone – she could not see the wood for the trees.

By focusing exclusively on what had to be done Bi-Polar Girl had lost the ability to raise her awareness above the level of her daily grind.

What can YOU do to ensure YOU
aren't sticking YOUR head in the sand?

The uncomfortable but unavoidable truth was this: Bi-Polar Girl was playing ostrich.

She had stuck her head in the sand.

She could not see *anything* any more, not even herself.

She had lost her discernment and a good part of her self-awareness. She had completely lost sight of what was really important to her.

Although she did not yet know it, Bi-Polar Girl was losing herself.

How do YOU cope when YOU
can't find any answers to YOUR questions?

What do YOU do when YOU feel
at war with YOURSELF?

Bi-Polar Girl had always been very articulate. She loved language and yet she could not talk to anybody about the slippery slope she was on.

She didn't know how to ask for help.

She wasn't even sure she needed help.

She didn't know anything any more.

She had no answers. Questions were all she had left.

Bi-Polar Girl felt she was at war with herself.

How do YOU feel when you realise you are sliding downwards, totally out of YOUR control?

Bi-Polar Girl was heading for a BIG crash.

She continued to struggle until finally it became impossible for her to carry on.

It would take a massive breakdown for Bi-Polar Girl to stop dead in her tracks.

It would take a total collapse for her to change tack altogether and learn how to use her energy and talents in a sustainable way.

It would take A LOT of pain.

Chapter 4
THE CRASH

Reaching the Inevitable

BI-POLAR GIRL

How did YOU feel when you were
diagnosed with bipolar disorder?

When Bi-Polar Girl eventually saw a psychiatrist he suggested that she try drugs different from the ones prescribed by her GP. He said Bi-Polar Girl was not just suffering from depression but from manic depression, also known as bipolar disorder.

This came as a nasty shock to Bi-Polar Girl because she had heard of manic depression before.

She had grown up with a father who had manic depression/ bipolar disorder and she HATED that illness. Her father's unpredictable and often violent behaviour had been very frightening to her as a child.

The thought of having the same condition made her feel like she was cracking up from the inside out.

How would YOU describe YOUR
reaction to bipolar disorder?

Bi-Polar Girl wanted to run away from the nasty, scary illness that was now making her life so bad. She desperately wanted to crawl out of her own body to escape the torment she was in.

Bi-Polar Girl felt trapped in a world of unbearable pain: physical (her body hurt all over), mental, emotional, and spiritual.

She felt as if she had found her own private version of hell.

Bi-Polar Girl wanted to run but she could not even move. She was completely stuck.

What knowledge do YOU
need to help YOU understand YOUR
bipolar disorder better?

The Crash

Bi-Polar Girl wanted desperately to understand what was happening to her so she struggled to read everything she could find on clinical depression and bipolar disorder.

This was very hard because her concentration had become so poor and her language processing such hard work that she could only read a few sentences at a time.

Bi-Polar Girl did learn a lot about her illness and it made it easier for her to cope with it. It also made it easier for her to talk to her family and friends about what was happening to her.

She could explain that she wasn't just feeling sad, or fed up, or under the weather.

What has been YOUR
experience with anti-depressants/
psychiatric medication?

The Crash

For the months that followed her first visit to the psychiatrist, Bi-Polar Girl tried sixteen different medications. Every time she thought her condition was improving she went back down again, each time feeling a little worse than before.

Not only did none of the drugs help her feel any better but some of them made her feel even worse. Her illness felt heavier and heavier, more and more difficult to live with.

Bi-Polar Girl's body had been filled with so many different medicines that the psychiatrist ordered her to stay off all medication for one month in order to give her body a chance to clear itself out.

On top of all that, she found that she was putting on a lot of weight: Bi-Polar Girl's body was also getting heavier. Things were not looking good.

What extreme emotions have YOU
experienced as a result of YOUR
bipolar disorder?

After three weeks without medication, Bi-Polar Girl reached the point where she wanted to kill herself and pulverise everything around her.

Bi-Polar Girl felt as if a huge rage was building up inside and she was ready to explode. She became highly agitated and could not stop herself from pacing back and forth.

One night, Bi-Polar Girl felt so destructive and so desperate that she became very scared and had herself admitted to the local psychiatric hospital.

Because she had been in psychiatric wards before, when visiting her father, Bi-Polar Girl was not afraid of hospitals. She was much more afraid of her illness.

What is YOUR experience of
being hospitalised?

Have YOU ever felt like YOU
wanted to die?

Bi-Polar Girl was hospitalised for a while and she tried other medications. Nothing seemed to work and Bi-Polar Girl gradually lost her fluency with thought and language.

Her brain felt like something had been short-circuited. Everything became more and more difficult. Everything hurt. Everything was too bright, or too loud, or too strong-smelling, or too strong-tasting.

Bi-Polar Girl reached the point where she could no longer function at all.

Bi-Polar Girl had one thought and one thought only: she wanted out; she wanted to die.

Chapter 5
PROGRESS AT LAST

Small Steps Forward

What do YOU know about
electroconvulsive therapy?

What is YOUR experience of
electroconvulsive therapy?

Having tried so many different medications without success, Bi-Polar Girl's psychiatrist suggested she might consider trying electroconvulsive therapy (ECT).

Bi-Polar Girl became even more scared.

She was terrified of ECT. She thought electroshock treatment sounded like torture.

She spoke to the ECT team at her local psychiatric hospital and felt a bit better after she was given a lot of information about ECT and was able to ask questions.

She decided to try ECT treatment. She was still nervous but she was also desperate.

If no medication worked for you,
would YOU consider ECT?

After the first ECT treatment, Bi-Polar Girl noticed that her brain was functioning slightly better, as if some light had come back in.

It felt good to be thinking, speaking, and reading more easily.

This was such a relief!

The ECT was definitely helping her and Bi-Polar Girl had two series of twelve ECT treatments.

The first treatments happened twice weekly, then weekly, then every other week.

If you have had ECT, how helpful
has it been for YOU?

What side effects have YOU
experienced from ECT?

Bi-Polar Girl was lucky. ECT made a big difference. She felt better and better and started believing that she would one day recover.

She was also very grateful because the whole ECT team was so friendly and supportive. Bi-Polar Girl was no longer afraid of ECT.

The ECT treatment had provided one other benefit: Bi-Polar Girl was now well enough to receive one-to-one support from the local mental health support unit. It was so good for her not to feel so utterly alone any more.

But there was one drawback: ECT had affected Bi-Polar Girl's memory. She soon noticed that she had trouble remembering events and people. Bi-Polar Girl put up with the disruption to her memory because NOTHING ELSE had given her any relief from her terrible symptoms and she had now been ill for over three years.

What is the first thing YOU like
doing when you feel better?

Bi-Polar Girl was happy to be able to cook again. She knew that eating well was important to her recovery.

When she felt really bad, Bi-Polar Girl could not even walk into the kitchen. It was as if she did not have any energy to give to food preparation.

In fact, the very thought of cooking used to make her feel worse. She used to eat very strangely, sometimes living on semolina for weeks!

So it felt good to enjoy tastes and smells, and to eat normally again.

Even life itself started to taste better.

What is the best *physical* part
of feeling better for YOU?

It also felt good for Bi-Polar Girl to have a shower again. When she felt very bad, Bi-Polar Girl could not step into the shower because the water felt like needles on her skin.

Just the thought of having a shower used to make her feel terrible.

But Bi-Polar Girl hated not being able to wash. She had always been a very hygienic person so it was hard for her not to feel clean any more. She hated the thought of becoming Body-Odour Girl!

It also felt good for her to do her hair again, and to put on 'going out' clothes (even if most of her wardrobe was now three sizes too small!).

On a really good day, she even managed to put on a bit of make-up.

When YOU feel very ill, how hard is it for YOU to leave the house?

How does physical exercise help YOU to feel better mentally?

It was good to go for a walk in the park again without feeling terrified of going through the front door.

Bi-Polar Girl could not believe she had been such a recluse during her long illness. She had not gone out of the house for months.

She was used to being an extrovert who enjoyed socialising and working as a member of a team, and she had always enjoyed nature. Not being able to go out had made Bi-Polar Girl feel very deprived – she had felt like a prisoner in her own skin.

The question now was: Would Bi-Polar Girl maintain her improvement without any further drugs?

Only time would tell.

What tells YOU that your mental health
is deteriorating (again)?

Some weeks later, after the ECT treatment had stopped, Bi-Polar Girl noticed that she wasn't feeling so good again.

She could still function reasonably well but her mood was gradually becoming darker. She felt the black clouds gathering again and self-destructive thoughts reappeared on her horizon.

Having been better for a while, this return to feeling awful made Bi-Polar Girl sad, angry, and frightened.

Bi-Polar Girl suddenly deteriorated very fast. She went back to see her psychiatrist in a hurry.

Things were bad AGAIN.

What relationship do YOU have
with YOUR psychiatrist?

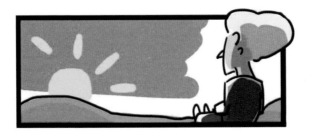

This time, her psychiatrist first suggested a combination of drugs to help Bi-Polar Girl remain stable. He then changed his mind and suggested another set of drugs.

Her psychiatrist had given her treatment a lot of thought and Bi-Polar Girl appreciated his efforts.

There was the possibility that the sun may shine on Bi-Polar Girl's horizon after all.

How much has YOUR physical
health suffered as a result of YOUR
bipolar disorder?

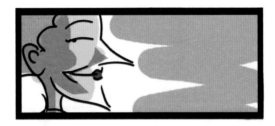

This time, the drugs worked.

The ECT had put Bi-Polar Girl's brain back on the rails and the drugs were stopping it from behaving like a runaway train.

This was brilliant news and Bi-Polar Girl started to feel hopeful again.

As she started to stabilise – beyond the immediate relief she had felt that the drugs were working – Bi-Polar Girl became aware of how battered her body had been during her long illness.

She also became painfully aware of all the things she could no longer do.

Chapter 6

THE POINT OF RESPONSIBILITY

Caring for Myself

What important decisions could YOU
take to support YOUR recovery?

Bi-Polar Girl understood that her medication could only do *some* of her recovery work – she would have to do the rest herself. So she took three important decisions:

1. She would focus her attention on rebuilding her physical health.

2. From now on, she would accept her limits without defining herself by her limitations.

3. She would laugh at her situation as much as she could without ever ignoring or dismissing her true feelings.

How has bipolar disorder
affected the way YOU eat?

Bi-Polar Girl had put on a lot of weight during her illness, due to the effects of the medication and a great deal of comfort eating.

She was not too concerned about the cosmetic aspect of her weight gain but she hated the sore back and painful knees that came from carrying too much weight.

Bi-Polar Girl had been on many diets throughout her life but this time she decided to change the way she ate for good. No diet – just eating differently.

The fact that she was now well enough to move and walk more frequently also helped Bi-Polar Girl feel better.

What could YOU clear out of
YOUR mind and out of YOUR life to
help YOUR recovery?

The drugs could only do so much and Bi-Polar Girl accepted that she must do some healing work too.

Bi-Polar Girl knew deep down that she needed to clear out a lot of things.

Many bad memories and negative feelings had come up during her long illness so she started doing some 'emotional clearance' work with her counsellor. Bi-Polar Girl understood that this sort of work required time but she was prepared to be patient. This was good because patience had never been one of her virtues!

Bi-Polar Girl also did some physical clearing out. She got rid of a lot of old clothes from her cupboards, and old papers and files from her office.

**What could YOU do to express YOURSELF
and/or share YOUR experience of
YOUR bipolar disorder?**

The Point of Responsibility

Bi-Polar Girl took another BIG decision: she would not 'play the shame card' any more. She would hide her condition no longer.

Bi-Polar Girl admitted to herself that she had been given a bipolar diagnosis a long time ago but had refused to accept it. She had fought against her illness so hard and for so long. From now on, she would speak about it and she would write about it too.

She started her own blog where she shared her experiences. Even though they could not possibly understand what she had been through, people were supportive. Their encouragement played a vital role in helping Bi-Polar Girl live with her condition successfully. There was a long way to go but she no longer travelled alone in secret and in shame.

What conversations could YOU have
to help YOU feel less isolated?

Some days Bi-Polar Girl enjoyed having telephone conversations again. After months and months of not even being able to answer the phone, it was wonderful speaking to old friends once more.

Bi-Polar Girl could even concentrate on listening to others again. Listening made her feel like her world was stretching beyond her own limitations. She could participate in other people's experiences and adventures. She could help her friends deal with *their* problems for a change.

Bi-Polar Girl also found that she was becoming more and more articulate in the way she described what was happening to her. She could now share her experiences with others in a way she had never done before.

Bi-Polar Girl recognised that what people say is true: a problem shared is a problem halved!

What could YOU do when YOU feel
too exhausted for anything?

Some days Bi-Polar Girl felt very tired all the time. All she wanted to do was sleep and sleep some more.

It didn't matter how long she slept at night, she still felt like dozing for hours on end.

Sometimes, all she wanted to do was stare into space. Bi-Polar Girl could stay silent for hours, as if the sound of her own voice was too much noise and speaking required too much effort.

Even when Bi-Polar Girl was awake her brain was asleep. So Bi-Polar Girl found pleasure in simple, repetitive tasks such as knitting. She became a very good knitter!

What could YOU do when the pressure builds up inside and YOU feel agitated?

Some days Bi-Polar Girl had energy to burn, so much so that she felt pressure building up inside her. She used those days to catch up on the work she hadn't been able to do before.

She picked up the vacuum cleaner and caught up with housework. She did paperwork and got up to date with office work.

She ran up and down the stairs in her house without a second thought, even though the previous day she had not even left her bedroom.

And Bi-Polar Girl sang to herself. She also spoke to herself out loud (which amused her husband!).

Bi-Polar Girl had bursts of activity. On those days, Bi-Polar Girl had great difficulty sleeping (even with the strong 'knock-out' effect of her evening medication).

What is YOUR favourite place to be
when YOU feel low on energy?

Some days she could not do very much so Bi-Polar Girl taught herself to enjoy sitting in bed, reading or writing. She encouraged herself to feel grateful for having a safe and comfortable place to be.

This was not easy for her because Bi-Polar Girl had to overcome strong condemning thoughts of laziness and worthlessness.

Bi-Polar Girl was used to working hard. This was how she had always valued herself so being unable to DO anything was very difficult for her.

BUT she also knew from painful experience that pushing against her illness only fed it her own strength and this was NOT a good idea.

And so Bi-Polar Girl started appreciating the importance of resting and recharging.

What do YOU do when YOU
feel lost and confused?

Some days Bi-Polar Girl had no idea where she was or where she was going. She felt like she was lost at sea.

Bi-Polar Girl longed for terra firma – for land where she could make plans and trust herself to follow them, to set goals and expect herself to reach them. Out on the ocean nothing went to plan, or so it seemed.

So when the current was too strong, Bi-Polar Girl learnt to let herself be carried by the sea. She learnt to Go with the Flow, and Flow with the Go.

She learnt to *let* things happen instead of always *making* them happen. She also learnt to let things be. Bi-Polar Girl was learning to become an experienced old 'sea dog'.

What do YOU do to stop YOURSELF
worrying about the future?

The Point of Responsibility

Some days Bi-Polar Girl wondered about the future. She had no idea what it would be like.

Sometimes Bi-Polar Girl really worried about what was going to happen next week, next month, next year, but she did not find this at all helpful.

So instead Bi-Polar Girl learnt to focus her attention on the present. She did her best in the moment. Even if her best was not always enough, she knew that doing what she could, whenever she could, was the best way forward.

Bi-Polar Girl knew she may not be able to control the future but she did have some influence on the present.

Bi-Polar Girl understood that the present was her only place of personal power.

What simple things give YOU pleasure?

Who/what could YOU take care of
to help with YOUR recovery?

Some days Bi-Polar Girl rediscovered the pleasure of simple things – such as feeding the cat. Taking care of another living creature somehow helped her to take better care of herself.

Watching her cat reminded Bi-Polar Girl that living need not be a constant fight, so she looked for moments of contentment in her own life.

Besides, the cat had always known when Bi-Polar Girl was unwell. It used to sit on her lap (or on her chest in bed) and look straight into her eyes, gently touching her chest (or her face) with its paw until Bi-Polar Girl responded.

Bi-Polar Girl was happy to have 'conversations' with her cat again.

What do YOU do to show YOUR
appreciation to those who love YOU?

The Point of Responsibility

Some days Bi-Polar Girl was well enough to go out for a meal with her husband. He had played such a crucial role in helping her come through her long illness.

He too had had a very difficult and painful time. Bi-Polar Girl knew that, in many ways, watching someone you love suffer is worse than suffering yourself.

Bi-Polar Girl felt very happy about being able to thank him for his unflinching support and she felt lucky having so much love in her life. She understood that she might not have survived without it.

For the first time, Bi-Polar Girl also understood the importance of accepting help from others. She used to think it was a selfish thing to do but now she thought about it differently. She now called it 'giving others the gift of giving'.

What role do YOUR friends play in
helping YOU with YOUR recovery?

Some days Bi-Polar Girl was well enough to socialise with some of her good friends. They too had played an important part in her recovery journey.

Bi-Polar Girl was grateful for the friendship of good people. She now knew that even very strong, independent people need the support, affection, and encouragement of others.

Bi-Polar Girl had always thought that 'being there for others' was important; she now knew that 'being there for yourself' and 'allowing others to be there for you' were equally important. Together they build a tripod of good equilibrium. Bi-Polar Girl now understood that equilibrium was vital to maintaining her own stability and balance.

For Bi-Polar Girl, good friends were a wonderful complementary medicine.

When YOU need it, what do YOU do to
ensure YOU recharge YOUR energy?

Some days Bi-Polar Girl felt the need to be alone. She did not want to see anybody; she did not want to speak to anybody. Socialising was out of the question.

Bi-Polar Girl learnt to treat those days as Renovation Days when she needed to step aside for a while to let her body do some internal repair work.

She learnt to enjoy those days.

Bi-Polar Girl stopped apologising for them and instead made sure that her loved ones understood that she was not rejecting them. On the contrary, she still loved them very much; it was just that she needed to 'go inside' for a while.

What makes YOU feel particularly
impatient and/or frustrated?

Some days Bi-Polar Girl felt very confused. Her brain seemed to move inside her head. Her thoughts were jumping all over the place. She didn't know WHAT was going on!

She could not say what was wrong because whatever it was did not stay still long enough for Bi-Polar Girl to put her finger on it.

On those days Bi-Polar Girl felt disorganised and she was also very clumsy. Many things got dropped, chipped, or broken. Her memory seemed a lot worse too so many other things got lost.

Very frustrating! But Bi-Polar Girl knew that, even if they kept coming back, those moments would not last forever. So she laughed at her own dingbat ways and focused her attention on being patient. This was a challenge because Bi-Polar Girl was used to being organised and efficient.

What new things do YOU like to
learn to help YOU feel better?

Some days her brain worked so well that Bi-Polar Girl could even teach herself new skills. She learnt to use her computer in new ways. This in turn helped her to communicate more easily with people who lived far away.

When she could learn something novel, Bi-Polar Girl felt like she was making real progress. She had spent such a long time re-learning what she had once done, or known, that she had often felt *mentally disabled* as well as *mentally ill*.

Sometimes she thought her brain had 'gone' forever. When these scary thoughts came along, she reminded herself that the brain was a plastic and highly flexible organ. The important thing was for her to keep a curious attitude and an open mind.

This way, Bi-Polar Girl would gradually recover her learning and understanding abilities.

What do YOU find particularly tiring?

Some days Bi-Polar Girl had enough energy to go to the local supermarket. She always found the store environment very tiring, what with the strip lighting, the noise, and all those people.

Being able to go food shopping was very important to Bi-Polar Girl. The more she could go out to buy fresh food, the easier it was for her to cook nutritional meals and the better it was for her body's health.

Bi-Polar Girl realised that her body was a very important ally in getting back her strength and stability. She no longer believed that mental illness was all in the head. She now knew that (to a significant degree) her mental health depended on – and was influenced by – her physical health.

What she put in her body made a difference to what came out of her brain.

What do YOU do to help YOU feel
less sorry for YOURSELF?

Some days Bi-Polar Girl felt totally fed up and frustrated with herself. All she could think of was that she wished she did not have bipolar disorder.

Bi-Polar Girl sometimes felt like her life had been blighted, wasted even, fighting this nebulous and yet ferocious illness.

BUT she no longer tried to deny those thoughts or suppress those feelings – she accepted them as they were. It was 'normal' for Bi-Polar Girl to feel sorry for herself sometimes. Bi-Polar Girl was human after all!

AND Bi-Polar Girl also knew that *allowing* 'poor me' thoughts and feelings was not the same as *wallowing* in them.

She learnt to let those thoughts and feelings pass *through* her without getting stuck to them.

Other than medication or ECT, what
treatment(s) have YOU found helpful?

Some days Bi-Polar Girl was lucky enough to be given acupuncture at her local psychiatric hospital.

The acupuncture treatment did not take the ocean away but it helped Bi-Polar Girl's body ride the bipolar waves.

Sometimes she felt very tired afterwards. Sometimes she felt energised. Sometimes it didn't make any difference the same day – only on the days that followed. Sometimes it made an immediate impact.

But it always helped – and without EVER having any side effects.

This made a big difference to Bi-Polar Girl because her medication was enough for her system to cope with (even if it was indispensable to Bi-Polar Girl's well-being).

Chapter 7

LOOKING TO THE FUTURE

Return to Hope

What is the funniest thing YOU can think of to help YOU laugh *with* YOUR illness?

What sort of future do YOU imagine for YOURSELF?

Over time Bi-Polar Girl began to accept the fluctuations of her condition and learnt to laugh at her ups and downs.

Bi-Polar Girl realised that by fighting her condition and her medication so hard and for so long, she had eventually experienced the equivalent of a violent volcanic eruption. Her breakdown had also been a 'break-wide-open'.

Bi-Polar Girl knew she had a stark choice: treat her illness as a total disaster OR recognise it as a powerful teacher that would no longer be ignored. She chose the latter.

And so Bi-Polar Girl laughed at herself WITH her illness. Together they giggled at her previous stubbornness and stupidity, chuckled at her dismantling herself and putting herself back together again, smiled at her forgiving herself for her past mistakes and her willingness to create a new future for herself.

What could YOU do to ensure YOU work *with* YOUR illness instead of against it?

Bi-Polar Girl did not pretend that her days were always good or even pleasant. She did not deny (or feel ashamed for) feeling bad BUT she did *focus her attention* as much as possible on feeling happy.

Bi-Polar Girl no longer tried to put a happy gloss on a miserable self because it did not work BUT she did *gently redirect* any unhappy thoughts towards happier ones. She now knew that being positive was not about being naive or unrealistic – it was about looking the present in the face while remaining hopeful for a better future.

Bi-Polar Girl learnt to EXPECT better days, better health, better wealth. There was no point in expecting the worst!

What do YOU need to do to ensure YOU
are aware of YOUR brain function?

What do YOU need to do to ensure YOU
are listening to YOUR body?

Bi-Polar Girl accepted that, from now on, she would have to keep a close eye on herself. She could no longer afford to ignore tiredness and pain signals.

She knew she would also need to take notice of the small changes (such as in her breathing or in her temper) that announce a rise into mania or a descent into depression. That way, she could 'nip them in the bud' (with medication or with other means such as deep breathing and relaxation) before they became unbearable.

Bi-Polar Girl was willing to treat her brain with respect and fascination rather than just as a malfunctioning piece of machinery that was prone to let her down.

She was happy to become her own doctor, working in close partnership with her psychiatrist.

What stops YOU from loving
YOURSELF unconditionally?

What stops you from seeing YOURSELF
as the star YOU really are?

Bi-Polar Girl was finally learning to love herself unconditionally, 'mental warts' and all.

She now understood that, even if she didn't shine every second of every day, she could still be a star in her own eyes.

Bi-Polar Girl knew she could have a happy life and a bright future. All she needed to do was:

1. Treat herself with kindness and compassion.

2. Acknowledge her unique gifts as well as her potentially debilitating condition.

3. Focus on what she loved doing and not just on what needed to be done.

4. Continue to treat her illness as an intelligent friend, not as a deadly enemy.

What would need to happen now for YOU to believe that YOU will one day be at peace with YOUR illness and with YOURSELF?

May YOU find YOUR way to YOUR place of peace where hope and laughter live side by side.

www.bi-polargirl.com

For more information and support regarding bipolar you can contact MDF The BiPolar Organisation, the national bipolar charity, telephone 0207 793 2600 or through their website www.mdf.org.uk